SOMETHING EXTRA TO THINK ABOUT

52 extra modern day parables
BY JIM COLLINS

Copyright © Jim Collins

The right of Jim Collins to be identified as author of this work has been asserted by him in accordance with the Copyright, Designs and Patents Act 1988

Published in 2015 by Verité CM for Jim Collins

All Rights Reserved. No part of this publication may be reproduced or transmitted in any form or by any means, electronic or mechanical including photocopying, recording, or any information storage and retrieval system, without permission in writing from the publisher.

Biblical quotations are taken from the Holy Bible, New International Version, Copyright © 1973, 1978, 1984 International Bible Society, used by permission of Zondervan Bible Publishers.

Other Biblical quotations are from the New King James Copyright © 1982 by Thomas Nelson, Inc.

The Message – The New Testament, Psalms and Proverbs – Copyright © 1993, 1994, 1995, 1996 by Eugene H. Peterson.

The Amplified Bible – Copyright @ 1954, 1958, 1962, 1964, 1965, 1987 by The Lockman Foundation.

ISBN: 978-1-910719-11-4

Cover design, typesetting and production management by Verité CM Ltd, Worthing, West Sussex UK +44 (0) 1903 241975

Book cover and internal pencil drawings by George Wellburn 'Scenic Keswick' – 2015

Printed in England

Contents

	Foreword	5
	Introduction	7
1	This New Year	8
2	Thinking of you	10
3	Completed work	12
4	Disappointment	14
5	Follow Me	16
6	I love you!	18
7	A Skip full	20
8	The peacock	22
9	The lion	24
10	The elephant	26
11	What is your vision?	28
12	Royal visit	30
13	It is finished	32
14	Keep on keeping on	34
15	Today	36
16	The ferry wake	38
17	Fixed gaze	40
18	Koi carp	42
19	Think about it	44
20	Mock exam	46
21	Imitators	48
22	Narrow lanes	50
23	X Rays	52
24	Just ask	54
25	Strength in our weakness	56

26	Denim alert!	58
27	Excuses	60
28	New Birth day	62
29	Who can I turn to?	64
30	Car recall	66
31	Commend or complain?	68
32	All things are possible	70
33	Shadows	72
34	Roots	74
35	New identity	76
36	Friends	78
37	What brings you joy?	80
38	Inconvenient interruptions	82
39	Weather warning!	84
40	Take a pause	86
41	Forever	88
42	Messages	90
43	Seasons	92
44	The Voice	94
45	Precious	96
46	Benefits	98
47	New home	100
48	Bullworker	102
49	Gifts	104
50	Cats eyes	106
51	Every step	108
52	Wishing or hoping?	110
	Other titles by Jim Collins	112

Foreword

It seems that the number of people expressing their faith continues to decline. Churches seem to be struggling with numbers and it is becoming harder and harder for them to survive.

But, at the same time, the 'From Your Parish' page continues to go from strength to strength with more and more news and events being published each week.

It is a home for all that is going on from the world of faith, and is one of the most popular pages of the paper. It is a running joke each week that the page produced is an 'award-winner', but I truly believe that it is, and a big part of that is Jim's thought for the week.

No matter what the subject matter is – Jim writes in such a way that engages you from the start. He manages to take what could be seen as simple everyday things and manages to extract a deeper meaning from them, and then puts the teachings of the Bible into a modern context.

His words are always readable and enjoyable, and he has demonstrated that he can provide a thought for the week on virtually any topic or subject matter.

Through the newspaper, these thoughts and his words are able to be transmitted to a wider audience.

You don't necessarily have to be religious to be interested in what Jim has to say. His words, thoughts, and teachings resonate just as much with those who don't believe in God as those who do.

Jim's thoughts are there to be dipped in and revisited and provide a sense of optimism and of a bright future.

They may just be the thought for the week, but they stay with you for a lot longer than that.

Daniel Clark, Herald Express

Introduction

Many years ago – Street Newspaper vendors would shout out "Extra, Extra – read all about it!" informing those passing by of their special issue paper with news that had not made the normal publishing schedule. This news would be sensational, important and the most up-to-date. (Today, we'd call it 'breaking news!')

Following on from my first book 'Something To Think About' – welcome to the '*EXTRA*' edition –'Something Extra To Think About.' Another compilation of 52 modern day parables, helping you to discover God's greater purpose in the 'everyday things of life.'

In using everyday experiences – that most of us will go through at some time – I hope this *EXTRA* will serve to bring to your remembrance God's word of hope, help and encouragement – in every situation of your life.

God desires to make himself known to each of us. He longs that we know Him as our Friend and LORD. As you turn the pages of this '*EXTRA*' you will read about 'life changing news.'

"Read all about it!" – and may you know the blessing of God's love, forgiveness and grace.

Jim Collins

This New Year

As our clocks strike midnight on December 31st, another year is over and a new one commences. A recent study revealed that 95% of British people will endeavour to keep some sort of 'New Year resolution.'

The top three resolutions were – to lose weight, get fit and eat more healthily. The list also included: to get out of the rut – read more books – save money and spend more time with people that matter.

At the beginning of this New Year – when many of us will be thinking about our plans and the changes we want to see in our lives – it's a good time to remind ourselves of the plans God has in mind for us.

The prophet Jeremiah wrote a letter to those in exile, reminding them of God's promise: "For I know the plans I have for you, declares the Lord, plans for welfare and not for evil, to give you a future and a hope." (Jeremiah 29:11)

King Solomon said "The heart of a man plans his way – but the Lord establishes his steps." (Proverbs 16:9 ESV Bible) When we put God's plans, above and before our plans and desires – God will grant us His ability and strength to do the things He asks of us.

When we seek and follow God's ways for our life; we can be confident like the apostle Paul who said of God – "He who began a good work in you will carry it on to completion…" (Philippians 1:6)

Resolutions can be made at any time – we don't have to wait for the start of a new year. "Those who plan what is good – show love and faithfulness." (Proverbs 14:22b)

As we step into this New Year: whatever lies ahead – when we seek God's plans and purpose for our lives as revealed in His word, we can rest secure in knowing that our times are in His hands.

EXTRA!

You don't have to wait for the start of a New Year to plan what is good.

Thinking of you

It was time to 'tidy up' and 'sort out' our roof space – which had become increasingly difficult to access due to the amount of items we continued to store in it.

Amidst Christmas decorations, jig-saw puzzles, suitcases and camping gear, I located my large cardboard box – full of greeting cards.

Inside, I found 'get well soon' cards sent to me when I was aged 10 – after I had my appendix removed. Also in my collection were cards for Birthdays, Valentine's Day (all sent from my wife) Wedding Anniversary, Father's Day and family Christmas cards. In addition there were others saying 'Sorry you are leaving' – 'Congratulations on your new job' and dozens of postcards.

I felt very encouraged that over the years, so many friends and family members have thought about me and sent me their love, prayers and greetings.

As I looked through these cards I was reminded of how much God thinks about us. David wrote in his Psalm – "How precious to me are your thoughts, O God! How vast is the sum of them! Were I to count them, they would outnumber the grains of sand" (Psalm 139:17-18)

David also thought about God. He said "On my bed I remember you; I think about you through the watches of the night." (Psalm 63:6)

When we think about God and His ways – He promises that He "will keep in perfect peace, those – whose mind is stayed on Him." (See Isaiah 26:3)

The apostle Paul said, "Each of you should look not only to your own interests, but also to the interests of others." (Philippians 2:4)

This week, just as God has you in His thoughts – think of someone who needs some comfort or encouragement, and find an opportunity to show them or to say – "I'm thinking of you."

EXTRA!

God has you in His thoughts all of the time

Completed work

On the news, I heard that a bridge over Glasgow's M8 which had been left unfinished since the 1970's – had finally been completed! The infamous 'Bridge to Nowhere' was left hanging in mid-air for decades after the shopping centre that it was meant to link, failed to materialise. It is now called the Anderston Footbridge which gives cyclists and pedestrians a route over the M8.

In our lives – there are many reasons why we may begin a work but don't get around to completing it. We may lose interest, get distracted by other tasks or realise that the job is beyond our own capability and needs the help of an expert to finish it.

We may be very inconsistent in finishing what we start – but God can be trusted to bring to completion all His purposes. Jesus came to earth to do all the works His Father (God) asked of Him. Jesus preached and lived the Good News – bringing healing and wholeness into people's lives. He gave His life and died on the Cross – so we could know His forgiveness for our sin and know the hope of heaven.

Jesus prayed to God His Father saying "I have brought you glory on earth by completing the work you gave me to do." (John 17:4) God will help us be good finishers in the things He calls us to do.

Paul wrote to the Church in Philippi saying he was confident that God "who began a good work in you will carry it on to completion until the day of Christ Jesus." (Philippians 1:5-6)

In Acts 20:24 – Paul shared "…I consider my life worth nothing to me, if only I may finish the race and complete the task the Lord Jesus has given me – the task of testifying the gospel of God's grace."

'Finishing' is not only important for the big projects in life – but also in every day matters. It may involve us doing a small practical task, or things like fulfilling promises and obligations made to family, friends and work colleagues – contacting that person because we've said "I'll get back to you."

This week; let us take some time to consider if there are any unfinished things in our lives, where with God's help and strength – we can complete them well.

EXTRA!

With God's help – we can complete unfinished tasks

Disappointment

Our daughter was talking about her disappointment after she had been informed she had not been successful in a job interview – but had come a very, very close second!

Each of us will continue to experience those sad feelings of displeasure that disappointment brings – as our hopes and dreams are shattered for various reasons.

There will be times when we give our very best, but it may still result in us working through the set-back of disappointment.

Disappointment can hit us from two directions. Firstly: when our desires and expectations fail, but also when others we trust and rely on – let us down.

It can also be very evident when role-models in society fail to live up to the standards we expect from them.

In the Bible – we can read how God comes to help us when we feel the strong emotion of disappointment creeping into our hearts and minds.

David declared in his psalm, "They cried to You and were saved; in You they trusted and were not disappointed." (Psalm 22:5)

The prophet Isaiah said – those who put their 'hope in the Lord' will not be disappointed (Isaiah 49:23b) and Paul the apostle reminds us "Hope does not disappoint us" (Romans 5:5)

When our trust is in God, we can leave it to Him to work out the 'bigger picture' for our lives. He knows the end from the beginning.

I had no quick-fix answers to give to my daughter as she shared her disappointment, but I told her I knew 'God – would give her His peace and perspective in this situation.' It's what God is great at doing and He will do the same for you as you call upon Him!

EXTRA!

The Lord knows the end from the beginning

Follow Me

With the huge increase in Social networking via the internet, the words 'following' and 'followers' have become very well used. As I watch the news on TV, read my newspapers and look at business adverts, I constantly read the invitation – "Follow us on Twitter!"

Twitter connects you to the latest stories, ideas, opinions and news from individuals and businesses – about the things you find interesting.

At the heart of Twitter are the small bursts of information called "Tweets." If you register – you will start to get 'followers' who are the people who receive and read your tweets.

You can follow celebrities, who may 'follow you' back – if they like your profile! Who and what we choose to spend our time following will have much influence upon our lives.

Jesus was walking by the Sea of Galilee, when he offered an invitation to Simon and his brother Andrew who were fishing.

"Come after Me [as disciples – letting Me be your Guide], follow Me, and I will make you fishers of men." (Matthew 4:19 – Amplified Bible) At once they left their nets and followed Jesus.

Walking on further, Jesus noticed two other brothers, James and John – who were in a boat with their father Zebedee – putting their nets right. He also called them, and they left their boat and their father, to follow Jesus and sided with Him.

Over 2000 years later, Jesus is still calling people going about their daily work – to "follow Him."

Those who accept that invitation will discover the greatest joy and purpose in life – that God wants to share His life with us (and work through us) as we choose to follow His way.

Open up a Bible: and as you read any of the four New Testament gospels – you will be able to 'follow Jesus' as He touches people's lives with His love, forgiveness, healing and hope.

Whatever you are facing and going through this week – when we trust God's Word of promise – He will be our Helper, Counsellor and Strength – for "Jesus Christ is the same yesterday and today and forever." (Hebrews 13:8)

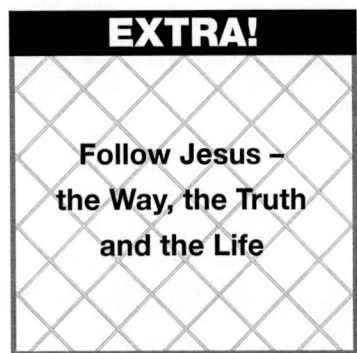

EXTRA!

Follow Jesus – the Way, the Truth and the Life

I love you!

Valentine's Day on February 14th is an extra opportunity to show the one you love just how much you care. My wife and I are rather inconsistent with giving gifts to each other on this day – but we always send a card. I have kept all of the Valentine's cards my wife has sent to me over the years.

It is estimated that approximately 1 billion Valentine cards are sent world-wide. It is thought that teachers will receive the most, followed by children, mothers, wives and finally sweet-hearts.

It's good to give and receive gifts like flowers and confectionery (and not just on Valentine's Day) to show love and share appreciation – but when the roses have withered and the chocolates have been consumed – the words in a card remain, to remind us 'we are loved.'

The Bible is 'Loves Greatest Story' – where God has written down for us how much we are loved and how we should love one another. We are reminded in 1 John 4:8 that… "God is love." The writer of this letter also explains how we know what love is. Jesus Christ laid down his life for us. (1 John 3:16)

Jesus said to His disciples, "Greater love has no-one than this, that one lay down his life for his friends…
(John 15:13-14)

Jesus was loved by God the Father – and He revealed and shared that same love towards His disciples. He told them to remain in His love. We can remain in Jesus' love – by obeying His commands. (John 15:9, 10)

We show our love for God by doing what He asks. Jesus gave a new commandment: "Love one another. As I have loved you, so you must love one another." (John 13:34) Also, our love for God and His Word needs to continue to increase and become stronger.

I found a web site that gave new ideas of how you can say "I love you." to that special person in your life. I liked the ones that showed that 'love needs to keep growing.' One read, "I love you more than I did yesterday but not more than I will tomorrow."

God's love towards us is eternal, incomparable, sacrificial and constant. Most importantly – it is 'for you' when you choose to receive it. "For God so loved the world that He gave his only Son, that whoever believes in Him should not perish but have eternal life." (ESV Bible)

EXTRA!

The Bible is 'Loves Greatest Story'

A Skip full

Many people use their garage to store everything in – but their car. We have managed to work it the other way. The car is parked in the garage, but as a result our shed is packed with items that come under the heading –'may be useful one day!'

On discovering the shed floor was rotting and needed replacing, my wife and I took the opportunity to 'rid the shed' of all the unnecessary things that had not been used for years. This amounted to a 'skip full.'

Making decisions on what must go, and what to keep can be difficult – but we easily packed the skip with wood, flower pots, metal poles, plastic buckets and bins in addition to many other old household units. It was very beneficial to have the clear out and gain the extra space.

Just as we fill up our sheds and garages with clutter – God reminds us in the Bible, of the things we fill our lives with – and need to rid ourselves of.

When Paul wrote to the Church in Ephesus he instructed them to "Get rid of all bitterness, rage and anger, brawling and slander, along with every form of malice." (Ephesians 4:31)

The apostle Peter added "Rid yourselves of all …deceit …hypocrisy …and envy." (1 Peter 2:1)

Paul gave an illustration by explaining the danger of how our wrong attitudes and behaviour affect us, and how (like yeast) they can influence others. He said – "…a little yeast works through the whole batch of dough. Get rid of the old yeast. (1 Corinthians 5:7)

As we choose to get rid of the old – we are to replace them with the ingredients and attitudes that God desires us to reveal to others, including kindness, compassion and forgiveness – just as Christ in God has forgiven us. (Ephesians 4:-32)

God doesn't just ask these things of us, and leave us to it. When we ask for His help in prayer – He enables and strengthens us to live His way.

EXTRA!

**Fill your life –
with the goodness
of God**

The Peacock

We were enjoying a family day at the Zoo. When it came to lunch time, we had our picnic in an outdoor area where we had a visit from a peahen – which walked around the tables fearlessly. Fortunately; a toddler chased it away regularly, allowing us to eat without interruption!

There were also several male peacocks wandering around – but we only saw one displaying his feathers. The long tail on an adult male peacock is called a 'train' and can reach 6 feet in length.

I was reminded of the saying 'As proud as a peacock.' This simile refers to the male peacock with its colourful tail that can be expanded like a fan to attract the female peahen. They pose and show off their striking – coloured feathers.

The Bible warns us of the danger of pride – which is evident when we hold an unduly high opinion of ourselves and our self worth. King Solomon wrote, "When pride comes, then comes disgrace, but with humility comes wisdom." (Proverbs 11:2)

Paul told the Church in Philippi "Do nothing out of selfish ambition or vain conceit, but in humility consider others better than yourselves." (Philippians 2:3) God has given everyone great gifts and talents – but in using them we should let another praise us – and not our own mouth.

The scriptures enable us to see and avoid the pitfalls of pride, but also reveal the right spirit of the word 'pride.'

Parents will feel pride in their newborn child – and then again in all their achievements. I recently told my grown up, married daughter – I was proud of her.

Paul the apostle said to the Church in Corinth, "I have great confidence in you; I take great pride in you."
(2 Corinthians 7:4)

Next time you see a peacock – instead of thinking of pride – think about the humility, attitude and example of Jesus: "Who being in very nature God, did not consider equality with God something to be grasped, but made himself nothing, taking the very nature of a servant."
(Philippians 2:5-11)

EXTRA!

Do nothing out of selfish ambition.

The Lion

As we walked around the Zoo we approached the lion enclosure. On the day we visited, we didn't get a close-up view of these 'king of the jungle' majestic creatures. They kept their distance! I was reminded of the saying 'as brave as a lion' – for they hold no fear of other predators.

Although lions are killers; they are also very social – living in their groups called 'prides.' The lionesses do the hunting while the lions have the task of giving them protection. They hunt in groups – and it is their group in addition to their own power, that give them the courage to even kill an elephant.

There is a proverb in the Bible that says "…the righteous are as bold as a lion." (Proverbs 28:1) It is God – who gives us His courage, to stand strong in times of fear.

When Moses died – God told Joshua (Moses' assistant) to get ready to cross the Jordan River. (Read the full story in Joshua 1:1-11) For the task of leading – God promised Joshua that He would be with him, and never leave or forsake him.

If you are walking a difficult road right now – or facing a problem where there appears to be no solution in sight – trust in God's words and take courage from His promise: "Do not be terrified; do not be discouraged, for the Lord your God will be with you wherever you go." (Joshua 1:9)

When 'Jesus walked on water' to meet his disciples who were in a boat experiencing windy weather conditions – He approached them saying three things "Take courage! It is I. Don't be afraid." (Mark 6:50) When Jesus climbed into the boat with them, the wind died down.

As a brave lion finds its 'courage for the fight' within its group – we can know boldness and strength for each challenge in life, by asking God to step in. King David- in his psalm of thanks declared: "Look to the Lord and His strength; seek His face always." (Psalm 105:4)

EXTRA!

You will find courage in God's promises

The Elephant

During our day at the Zoo, we had our cameras ready to take interesting pictures of the animals. We caught up with the elephant for a photo shoot while she was in her house. It is said that 'an elephant never forgets'– they have an excellent memory.

Compared to the human brain – the elephant's is denser and the temporal lobes associated to memory are more developed, and because their lobes have more foldings – they can store more information.

Researchers say; that a big part of an elephant's survival, is because of its remarkable recall power. Three elephant herds that were studied during a drought were able to recall their routes to other food and water sources when their usual areas dried up.

The Bible speaks much about remembrance and guides us on 'how to remember.'

When Moses reminded God's people concerning the Ten Commandments he said "These commandments …are to be upon your hearts. Impress them on your children. Talk about them … tie them as symbols on your hands …write them on the door frames of your houses…" (Deuteronomy 6:5-9) By doing this, God's people would not forget how they should live and behave.

When things are going bad, it's harder to recall the good times. When we are in need, it can be difficult to remember past blessings and provision – that God gave to us in His love, mercy and faithfulness.

The psalmist in his time of distress proclaimed "I will remember the deeds of the Lord; yes I will remember your miracles of long ago. I will meditate on all your works and consider all your mighty deeds." (Psalm 77:11-12)

The apostle Peter had been reminding believers of the importance of faith …goodness …self control …kindness and love. He went on to say, "So I will always remind you of these things, even though you know them… I think it is right to refresh your memory… and I will make every effort to see that after my departure you will always be able to remember these things." (2 Peter 1:3-15) Peter was dedicated to helping people remember, the very great and precious promises of God.

When we read and put our trust in God's word – we will remind ourselves that 'God is able.' Nothing is too difficult for Him!

EXTRA!

**Never forget –
God is loving,
faithful and merciful**

What is your vision?

My wife and I were visiting the city of Bath for a few days holiday. One day we took the Skyline Sightseeing bus, and got off at a stop – so we could look around Prior Park Landscape Garden. Looking through the leaflet we were given, I read about the story of one man's vision… Ralph Allen.

If you posted a letter in the early 1700s, it could take weeks to arrive at its destination – if ever. In 1720, Ralph Allen created Britain's first efficient postal system. He made his fortune – and invested in the nearby stone quarries. He used the stone to build Prior Park as a dramatic 'show house.' He wanted a building that would show the properties of Bath stone as a building material. It was described in 1788 as 'a noble seat which sees all of Bath and which was built for all of Bath to see.'

Many of the prominent buildings in Bath were then constructed from the honey-coloured stone. Over 200 years after Ralph Allen's death – visitors can still marvel at the magnificent views of Bath from this gem of a house and garden. His vision outlived him, and was passed on for future generations to enjoy.

This reminded me that God made all of us to have vision for our lives. He created the world in the beginning, and today – He continues to use us in creative ways to do His will and work.

The blessings and benefits of good inventions, medical research, and modern technology have all come from God – in that He is the One who made us with visionary minds and the ability to think.

David the Psalmist said to God "I praise You because I am fearfully and wonderfully made; your works are wonderful, I know that full well." (Psalm 139:14)

When we seek God in prayer and by reading the Bible, He will reveal to us His vision – for our lives. The Message Bible puts Proverbs 29:18 like this – "If people can't see what God is doing, they stumble all over themselves; but when they attend to what He reveals, they are most blessed." God wants to put into our minds – ideas and ways in which we can serve and help others and bring honour to Him.

This week, let us think about the things we put our time and attention to – and ask ourselves how the results of our efforts could outlive us – and with God's help and vision, be a benefit to future generations.

EXTRA!

God uses us in 'creative ways' to do His work

Royal visit

I was looking through my photograph albums and came across pictures I had taken when the Queen and Duke of Edinburgh visited Brixham in July 1988.

I recall in preparation of the Royal visit, the railings around the harbour had been repainted and the quayside was looking very clean and tidy.

A huge crowd gathered to welcome the Queen and Duke, who were transported to the harbour side by barge – from the Royal Yacht 'Britannia' which was anchored in Torbay.

Unfortunately, the day was misty and dull – but the weather did not dampen the enthusiasm and excitement of the waiting multitude as the Royal visitors stepped onto Brixham Quay.

The Bible records in detail the events of Palm Sunday – the day when King Jesus entered the City of Jerusalem. Kings usually rode in wheeled vehicles – but Jesus made his journey on a colt.

His coming visit was foretold over 500 years before by Zechariah the prophet. "Shout and cheer, Daughter Zion! Raise the roof, Daughter Jerusalem! Your King is coming! A good king who makes all things right, a humble king riding on a donkey, a mere colt of a donkey." (Zechariah 9:9 – The Message Bible)

The crowds that went ahead of King Jesus and those that followed shouted, "Hosanna (which means save!) to the Son of David! Blessed is He who comes in the name of the Lord." Matthew 21:8-9)

Jesus is King of kings and Lord of lords – the awesome God – the great King over all the earth and He reigns over the nations (see Psalm 47: 2, 8)

On Palm Sunday; the multitudes laid down their coats on the road, and broke off branches to wave – to welcome and worship Jesus – the King who had come to them.

Today and each day – Jesus wants us to experience that same joy in knowing Him as King of our lives. He is the One who still saves, and walks beside us – giving us His hope and guiding our every step.

EXTRA!

Jesus is King of kings – Sovereign over all!

It is finished!

I recently completed my studies for a NVQ in Cleaning. Over a period of 6 months, I answered questions, did research and was observed (sometimes on camera) while doing my work. It was a very beneficial Course – sharing with others, exchanging ideas and learning new things together. I recall how good it felt as I concluded the last observation and my NVQ work was now 'finished.' I sent a text to my wife saying – "NVQ – all done and dusted!"

On Good Friday – we remember that Jesus finished the work His Father sent Him to do. As Jesus hung on the cross He said -"It is finished." With that He bowed his head and gave up his spirit. (John 19:30)

On Good Friday – Jesus was falsely accused. He was mocked, beaten, spat upon, whipped and led away to be crucified. As Jesus died, darkness came over the whole land as the sun stopped shining. The earth shook and rocks split.

It was on that dark and cruel day; when the hopes of many were shattered – that Jesus 'finished' His work so that sinful mankind could be reconciled to God.

In His life – Jesus pointed the way to God and taught us how to live. Through His death on the cross for our sinfulness, He made the only way possible – for us to receive His forgiveness, mercy and grace.

On Good Friday, Jesus died – so we could have new life in relationship with God. Jesus was rejected by men – but He turned the cross into a place of acceptance.

"For Christ died for sins once for all, the righteous for the unrighteous to bring you to God." (1 Peter 3:18a)

The work that Jesus finished takes us from Good Friday to Easter Sunday. Just as Jesus promised – He rose from the dead after three days. (Mark 10:32-34) Both the cross and the grave of Christ are empty – and Jesus is alive!

When we trust in Christ's finished work we can rejoice like Peter the apostle, who proclaimed that God in His great mercy – "has given us new birth into a living hope through the resurrection of Jesus Christ from the dead, and into an inheritance that can never perish, spoil or fade – kept in heaven for you." (1 Peter 1:3-4)

> **EXTRA!**
>
> Jesus finished the work His Father sent Him to do

Keep on keeping on

I was watching the 160th Oxford and Cambridge boat race on the TV. To date, Cambridge lead with 81 wins and Oxford have 78. There has been one draw.

The 4.2 mile course of River Thames between Putney and Mortlake, provides the challenge for the two rowing teams to put to the test all the hard training they have done during the year. Sadly for Cambridge in 2014 – their number 2 rower was briefly unseated following a clash of oars, and Oxford simply cruised away to victory by 11 lengths.

When this incident happened, the TV commentator explained how vital it would be for the Cambridge Cox to keep his team going as only he could see the distance that Oxford were ahead. With victory way out of sight – he needed great perseverance to encourage his crew just to complete the race.

After the race the unseated Cambridge rower commented, "I'm proud of the guys for the way they kept going, and I'll be up for the fight next year. You never want to lose like that, but you keep your head high and move on."

Perseverance is that quality that makes us persistent in doing something – despite difficulty or delay in achieving success.

When the apostle Paul wrote to the believers in Rome he explained that they could rejoice; even in their suffering – because they knew that suffering produces perseverance, and perseverance produces character, which in turn leads to hope that does not disappoint. (Read Romans 5:3-5)

Jesus' brother James reminds us to "Consider it pure joy my brothers, whenever you face trials of many kinds, because you know that the testing of your faith develops perseverance. Perseverance must finish its work so that you may be mature and complete, not lacking anything. (James 1:2-4)

Job, in all his suffering and troubles; persevered – and God brought about an outcome that revealed His compassion and mercy. The Lord blessed the latter part of Job's life more than the first. (Read Job 42:12-17)

Don't give up or give in – to the tough challenge you may be facing today. Be encouraged by the blessing that Paul gave to the Church of the Thessalonians when they needed to stand firm and be strengthened. "May the Lord direct your hearts into God's love and Christ's perseverance." (2 Thessalonians 3:5)

> **EXTRA!**
>
> The testing of your faith develops perseverance

Today

Our daughter and son in law live in Wales – and when we go and see them, we enjoy going on walks together or visiting new places of interest. It was during a late spring visit we decided to go to Tredegar House. This is a late 17th Century Mansion. The house was home to one of the greatest Welsh families – the Morgan's.

Walking around the house – you step back in time. In the dining room – the table was laid out for a wedding feast. The many paintings on the walls revealed characters and scenes from over the centuries.

In one room there was a box of hats to try on. Choosing our headwear – we took photos of ourselves with our 'historic look.'

It was good to be able to 're-live history', but it also reminded me of the importance of living for 'today' – (this very time and moment as you read these words)

Some of us may be living with regrets from the past, while others fear tomorrow and the future for themselves and their children. God made us to live one day at a time.

When Jesus taught his disciples to pray, He used the words "Give us 'today' our daily bread." (Read Matthew 6:9-13) Jesus also said – "…do not worry about tomorrow, for tomorrow will worry about itself. Each day has enough trouble of its own." (Matthew 6:34)

David the psalmist practiced this principle when he prayed "Morning by morning, O Lord you hear my voice; morning by morning I lay my requests before you and wait in expectation." (Psalm 5:3)

David also spoke of God – as the One who "daily bears our burdens." (Psalm 68:19)

If we are feeling guilt or shame from wrong decisions and choices in the past – God forgives us when we ask Him. If tomorrow is too much to handle, God promises that His grace and enabling presence will be sufficient for us as we trust all things to Him.

Whatever you are going through – Today, is the beginning of the rest of your life. Each day, God offers fresh hope and help.

EXTRA!

Yesterday has gone – Today is a fresh start

16

The Ferry wake

In my working life, I have made hundreds of crossings of the River Dart via the Ferry – on my journey from Brixham to Dartmouth. Many times, I would arrive on the slipway to discover the ferry was full – but as I rode a motor cycle, I was able to squeeze in behind the last car and the closing gate.

It was on these journeys; I would look behind and observe the wake, the ferry had made in the water. The wake opened wide, and pushed small waves to the sides of the river bank. The trip only takes about 3 minutes – but by the time you reach the other side, and the ferry slows down to land – the wake has almost disappeared.

The 'open wake' reminded me of times in our lives when we have opportunities that open up before us, and we need to take them – before the wake closes over and the moment is lost.

The Bible reveals God's plan and purpose for us in life – and as we trust Him – He will bring about every opportunity that we need to do His will and to meet our daily needs. God said to His people in exile –"For I know the plans I have for you… plans to prosper you and not to harm you, plans to give you a hope and a future." (Jeremiah 29:11)

Solomon wrote in Proverbs 16:3 – "Commit to the Lord whatever you do, and your plans will succeed."

As we do the same – God will guide us in our decisions – help us in every situation and help us discern what opportunities are best.

We will all experience times when we feel regret over lost opportunities in the past; when doors have been firmly shut on our hopes and dreams.

Whether our missed opportunities have come from wrong choices we have made, or from circumstances beyond our control, remember that God – is the God of new opportunity. "…His compassions never fail. They are new every morning. Great is His faithfulness." (Read Lamentations 3:22-23)

God's Word also instructs us that we are to look for occasions where we can encourage and help others. The apostle Paul wrote "…as we have opportunity, let us do good to all people…." (Galatians 6:10)

EXTRA!

God – the God of new opportunity!

17

Fixed gaze

As I looked out into our back garden, I observed one of the neighbourhood cats sitting a short distance away from our wall – just staring at it! The cat was motionless and kept a fixed gaze. It was probably looking at snails hiding in the gaps between the stones.

That same week, I saw a seagull standing on our shed roof; and like the cat – it was motionless – and just staring down at the roof felt. (No sight of any snails this time!)

Whatever the reasons were for their 'prolonged peering' it reminded me that we need to consider carefully what we allow our eyes to stare or gaze upon.

A stare is when we look at someone or something – for a long amount of time – wide eyed and with concentration.

The Bible tells us in 2 Samuel chapter 11 – what happened to King David when he looked out from his own palace. From the roof, he saw Bathsheba bathing.

David broke the '2 second rule' when his glimpse became a stare – which then turned into a 'longing' for him to seek after Bathsheba. David's prolonged and intentional look led him to commit adultery, which then led him to murder and a cover up scheme.

God reminds us in His Word; to keep our eyes and focus on Him – always, and in all situations. The prophet Micah declared "Therefore I will look to the Lord; I will wait for the God of my salvation; My God will hear me." (Micah 7:7) God will hear and help us – when we call and look to Him in times of temptation, crisis or fear.

In the book of Hebrews, the writer gives us a picture of life being like a race. It is marked out for us – but it has to be run with perseverance. To enable us to do that, we have to "…fix our eyes on Jesus, the author and perfector of our faith…" (Hebrews 12:1-2)

Just as an athlete keeps looking forward when running – "Let your eyes look straight ahead, fix your gaze directly before you." (Proverbs 4:25-27) The Message Bible goes on to say – "Watch your step, and the road will stretch out smooth before you. Look neither right nor left; leave evil in the dust."

Whatever we face this week – as we 'fix our gaze on Jesus' and consider Him… He promises that we will not grow weary or lose heart." (Hebrews 12:3)

EXTRA!

Keep your eyes on Jesus

Koi carp

Some years ago, when my wife and I celebrated our 25th Wedding Anniversary – we bought ourselves a rather different present to mark the occasion. We visited a garden centre and came home with a 4 inch Koi Carp, to put in our garden pond. It was silver in colour and we named it 'Silver' to remember our special anniversary.

It was the only Koi Carp in the pond – and the other goldfish were of similar size.

After a few years – we noticed that Silver was increasing in size – much faster than the other goldfish. I had long thought that goldfish only grew to the size of their pond or tank. On further reading – I discovered – if a goldfish is properly cared for, it will not stop growing. In fact; most fish are 'indeterminate growers' – that means unlike humans, they grow until they die.

The size of pond does not restrict the final size of a koi carp – but rather the rate which it gets there.

Watching our pond fish, reminded me that God tells us in His word about areas of our life where we should be growing – and continue to grow day by day.

Paul's prayer for the people in Colosse was that they "bear fruit in every good work – growing in the knowledge of God." (Colossians 1:10)

John the Baptist said of Jesus – "He must increase, but I must decrease." (John 3:30) The Amplified Bible adds – Jesus "must grow more prominent" in us. To continue to grow in our faith – we must be obedient to what God asks of us in His word.

I took the opportunity at work to study for a NVQ Cleaning qualification. I think I can clean reasonably well – but I also know I can improve! We all need to 'remain teachable' to continue to grow – and to learn new skills.

When the apostle Paul wrote to the Church of the Thessalonians – he thanked God, as he noticed "their faith was growing more and more – and their love for each other was increasing." (2 Thessalonians 1:3)

Whether it is faith, love, patience, kindness, forgiveness, generosity, caring… when we seek and trust God, He will enable these characteristics to grow in us – in increasing measure – every day of our lives!

EXTRA!

Keep learning
Keep growing

19

Think about it

The aim of *"Something To Think About"* articles is to enable us to think further about a topic or aspect of life and to discover what God thinks and says about it.

I read in an article that 'all our thinking is done by electricity and chemicals.' When we think, laugh, see or move – it's because tiny chemical and electrical signals are racing between neurons (which are microscopic cells – and the brain contains about 100 billion of them)

Jesus was great at getting people to 'think for themselves' about the heart of an issue or situation.

On several occasions He answered people's questions – by asking them a question. In doing so; He drew out their true motives, as He encouraged them to trust Him and God His Father in all things.

One day an expert in the law tried to test Jesus by asking, "Teacher, what must I do to inherit eternal life?" Instead of giving a direct answer, Jesus replied, "What is written in the law? How do you read it?" (Read Luke 10:25-37)

What we think about is very important. Many years ago I heard a sermon where the preacher opened with the words "A man is not what he thinks he is. But what he thinks – he is!" Our thoughts will determine our behaviour, actions and re-actions.

The shepherd and prophet Amos spoke of the Lord God Almighty – as being the One who "reveals His thoughts to man." (Amos 4:13) As we read God's word, we discover what is on His mind and heart for us.

We all have times when anxious and negative thoughts just won't move from our minds. The more we ponder on them – they can cause us to worry more.

The apostle Paul said "Do not be anxious about anything, but in everything, by prayer and petition, with thanksgiving, present your requests to God. And the peace of God, which transcends all understanding, will guard your hearts and your minds in Christ Jesus. Finally… whatever is true – noble – right – pure – lovely – admirable – excellent or praiseworthy – think about such things." (Philippians 4:6-7)

EXTRA!

Our thoughts will determine our behaviour

Mock Exam

It was mock exam time at the College where I invigilate. A mock exam offers students a 'trial run' for the main event, giving them the opportunity to experience exam conditions and discipline – and to gauge how they will do in the actual exam. The result of the mock exam will highlight areas for further study – so students can improve on their grades.

During mock exams, students sometimes ask the Invigilators to explain the meaning of a word, or seek clarification on the question. We have to remind them (like in a real exam) we cannot offer hints towards the answer or guide them in any way.

It is during these times I am reminded that for many things 'in life – there is no trial run.' Life is the real exam! – where even with the experience and advice from others, we will still have times when we don't understand what is going on – and answers to our questions are hard to find.

However: in life, God is our helper and guide. We can call upon Him at any time and He will come alongside us. The psalmist declared "The Lord is with me; He is my helper. (Psalm 118:7)

The writer of Hebrews knew God would never leave or forsake him and was able to say with confidence "The Lord is my helper; I will not be afraid." (Hebrews 13:5-6)

King David wanted God to be his teacher and guide. He prayed, "Show me your ways, O Lord, teach me your paths; guide me in your truth and teach me, for you are God my Saviour, and my hope is in you all day long." (Psalm 25:4-5)

Are you in need of some direction, encouragement to persevere or hope for the future? The commands and promises in God's Word, will guide us in making good and right decisions in life. When you call on Him – you will discover that 'He is an ever present help in trouble'. (Psalm 46:1)

> **EXTRA!**
>
> When we have more questions than answers – God is our Helper and Guide

Imitators

From my early teens – I've enjoyed hearing performers who are able to imitate the voice and mannerisms of others. They must spend hours observing and listening to the person they want to copy.

I have to confess; Frank Spencer (acted by Michael Crawford in the comedy series *"Some mothers do 'ave 'em"* from the 1970's) was someone I impersonated. 'Frank' could also be recognised by copying his many mannerisms – without saying a word!

I also enjoyed watching the TV show "Stars in their eyes" where contestants would impersonate showbiz stars. The catch-phrase of the programme was "Tonight… I'm going to be…." This show was mainly based on a sound-alike, but they would also dress up, and be made up to look as close as possible to the singer they were impersonating.

This aspect of copying and imitating is a theme that God addresses in His word.

The apostle Paul said to the believers in Ephesus – "Be imitators of God, therefore, as dearly loved children and live a life of love, just as Christ loved us and gave himself up for us… (Ephesians 5:1)

Jesus calls us to model our lives on His will and purposes, so our example will influence those we meet day by day.

Just as a mimic would need to practice hard to work on their voice impression – "we become imitators of God as we obey (put into practice) what we read in His Word."

The apostle Paul used his life to imitate and follow Christ. When he was cursed – he blessed, when persecuted – he endured it – when slandered, he answered kindly. (1 Corinthians 4:12-13)

In the letter of 3 John 11 – we read "Dear friend, do not imitate what is evil but what is good…" As we seek to imitate God – and do what Jesus would do – He gives His power and strength to help us.

EXTRA!

Be imitators of God
- Live a life of love

Narrow lanes

One of the first things I noticed when I moved from Reading to Brixham was the challenge of driving on narrow Devon lanes.

Many of us have had that experience of needing to stop… and to check there is sufficient road width for two vehicles to pass. At times; you may have to open the car window to pull the mirror in – to make extra space.

It's not just the offside you have to watch. The 'nearside hedgerow' can put a pinstripe down the side of your car and put mud on the tyre walls – if you don't observe all around!

If you choose main routes to avoid the country roads – it may make your journey longer – and some destinations can only be reached by carefully navigating narrow lanes.

Towards the end of His Sermon on the Mount; Jesus taught His disciples a very important lesson – using an illustration of a narrow road. He told them "Enter through the narrow gate…. small is the gate and narrow the road that leads to life…" (Matthew 7:13-14)

Jesus himself is the Gate to Life. He said "I tell you the truth; I am the gate for the sheep… whoever enters through Me will be saved. He will come in and go out, and find pasture." (John 10:8-9)

Following Jesus is not an easy road. Many times in the Bible, Jesus explains about the cost of being a disciple. The narrow road is one where we seek God's will for our lives, and commit to doing whatever He says – even when it is difficult.

God is there for us on the narrow road – keeping and watching over us, on every step of life's journey.

Jesus said "I have come that you may have life, and have it to the full." (John 10:10b) When we choose to walk God's Way – and not take the broad gate to the broad road – we will know fulfilment and contentment in life.

The paradox of walking God's narrow road is: when we do – we will know the love of Christ which is wide, long, high and deep – and the God who walks with us, is able to do immeasurably more than we could ask or imagine." (Ephesians 3:18-20)

> **EXTRA!**
>
> Small is the gate and narrow the road that leads to life. Don't miss it!

23

X – Rays

I was experiencing some continued difficulties with my voice going hoarse – especially after I had been singing. My doctor sent me for some tests, which included taking an X-ray of my chest.

X-rays were discovered in 1895 by a German scientist named Wilhelm Conrad Roentgen, when he was experimenting in his lab with tubes similar to our fluorescent lamps. He evacuated the tube of all air, filled it with a special gas, and passed a high electric voltage through it. The tube produced a green coloured light. He was surprised to see the light penetrate through his flesh; and he could actually see the outlines of the bones in his hands on a film he had taped to a wall.

Roentgen had no idea how the rays worked – so he named them X-rays, with the X to signify they were unknown.

An X-ray shows what is going on 'inside' our body. It reminded me that God fully knows and understands what is going on 'inside of us.'

God is Omniscient – which means He is all knowing, of the past, present and future. What is hidden from human sight is still known by God – our thinking, motives, and every emotion. God knows us better than we know ourselves.

The work that God wants to do in us – starts with Him changing us on the inside. "Man looks at the outward appearance, but the Lord looks at the heart." (1 Samuel 16:7b)

Jesus said to the teachers of the law and the Pharisees, "You clean the outside of the cup, and dish, but inside they are full of greed and self-indulgence… First clean the inside of the cup and dish, and then the outside also will be clean." (Matthew 23:25-26)

Just as X-rays reveal things inside us that are causing problems – God's Word reveals; that attitudes within us like envy, hatred, selfish ambition and unforgiveness – will cause us and others harm and pain. When we seek God, He can bring His healing to all these things that arise within us.

The psalmist prayed "Search me, O God, and know my heart; test me and know my thoughts. See if there is any offensive way in me; and lead me in the way everlasting." (Psalm 139:23-24)

EXTRA!

The Lord looks at the heart

24

Just ask

Some years ago, a well known car breakdown service used the words "Just Ask" as a logo on their membership cards. One phone call and a request – would send a roadside mechanic to help get your car problem sorted.

One day, I inadvertently selected an option on my computer and a new tool bar appeared on my screen, which I could not get rid of. I spent much time trying to get my system back to how it was – but without success, so I did an Internet search, asking for the remedy. One short Youtube clip later, and after following the instructions – my computer was back to normal.

The Bible is packed with examples of people who called on God and asked for His help, guidance and provision – and also asked Him questions about the big issues in life.

God longs that we call on Him. The things we are to ask in Jesus' Name – are to bring glory to God the Father. (See John 14:13)

When Solomon became King (as a little child) he did not ask God for long life, or wealth for himself, or death for his enemies.

His prayer was "...so give your servant a discerning heart to govern your people and to distinguish between right and wrong." (See 1 Kings 3:7-12) God was pleased that Solomon asked for this and did what he asked.

Jesus' brother James said, "If any of you lacks wisdom, he should ask God, who gives generously to all without finding fault; and it will be given to him." (James 1:5) James added that we are to ask without doubting or wavering. God is faithful and true to His Word!

God always listens to our prayers. David the psalmist declared, "...the Lord will hear when I call to Him." (Psalm 4:3b)

When we desire to love and obey God and choose His ways – we will have confidence when we pray. The writer of 1 John reminds us: "We're able to stretch our hands out and receive what we asked for because we're doing what He said, doing what pleases Him." (1 John 3:22 – The Message Bible)

EXTRA!

The Lord hears when we call to Him

Strength in our weakness

It was a great shock for tennis fans when Rafael Nadal was knocked out in a first round match of the Wimbledon Lawn Tennis Championships. He responded by saying "It's tough losing in the first round but life continues…" He added, "talking about my knee injury is an excuse and I don't want to use excuses."

All of us have experienced times of losing and failure – it's part of life. However; viewed in the right way – failure can teach us many lessons that will help us to 'persevere and press on' when things are not going as we hoped.

I heard about a top girls school that was planning a 'failure week' – to teach pupils to embrace risk, build resilience and learn from their mistakes.

Emphasis was on the value of 'having a go' rather than playing it safe and perhaps achieving less. The Head Teacher commented that she wanted to show "it was completely acceptable and normal not to succeed at times in life."

Many characters in the Bible went through experiences of failure as they sought to follow God and live for Him.

Peter, a disciple of Jesus – failed! When Jesus was arrested – Peter followed Him at a distance, denied Him three times and ended up saying "I don't know the man." (Matthew 26:71-72)

There is much more to Peter's story… but he learnt from his failures! The outcome was – Jesus restored him and he was used in teaching and preaching in the early Church.

The apostle Paul wrote to the Church in Corinth reminding them; that although they had the treasure of the gospel of Christ to share – it was in jars of clay.

Being human, we are like jars of clay – fragile and prone to weakness and brokenness, but when we put our faith and trust in God, He can use each of us – even in our weakness and failure, to reveal that this all surpassing power is from Him and not from us. (2 Corinthians 4:7)

Paul saw hope and a positive aspect in each difficulty, and went on to say- "We are hard pressed on every side, but not crushed; perplexed, but not in despair, persecuted but not abandoned; struck down, but not destroyed." (2 Corinthians 4:8-10)

We also, can be assured that when we ask for God's help – His power will enable us to feel strength in our weakness and His blessing in our failure.

EXTRA!

God's power is made perfect in weakness

Denim alert!

When I'm buying a pair of jeans – I've got used to the fact that many of the designs I like will also be stone washed – which gives a new garment that 'worn-out' appearance.

One of my purchases had the following warning label in them. "Denim alert. Colour may transfer to other garments and upholstery!" One day, I noticed that both my knees were blue – as if I had bruised them. I realised, the dye from my jeans had permeated through to my skin.

This reminded me that Jesus taught His disciples in the Sermon on the Mount about God's Kingdom and values – so as they lived God's way, His love, joy, peace and forgiveness… would permeate through them, to everyone they met in their daily lives.

Today, even though we may fail and fall, God in His grace and mercy still desires to use us – to make His will and purposes known to others. We make God known when we choose to follow Him and model His characteristics in all of our ways.

The things we read and images we look at – will influence our thinking, which in turn will affect our words, actions and behaviour. The apostle Paul warned that sinfulness and immorality was like a little yeast – working through the whole batch of dough. (1 Corinthians 5:6)

Our choices and what we example, can influence and 'transfer' to others – for good or bad.

As we read and put into practice God's word (which includes commands and promises) – He will use our lives to be salt and light in the world. (Matthew 5:13-14)

As we say 'no' to what we want and 'yes' to what God wants – His love, grace and blessing will permeate and spread through us to others.

> **EXTRA!**
>
> Jesus makes himself known to others through us – as we live for Him

Excuses

I heard on the news; some excuses that people gave for not purchasing a TV licence. The reasons given to Officials by evaders included: a home owner said they did not think they had to pay their TV licence fee, because they claimed their pet was related to one of the Queen's dogs! Another revealed- they thought a licence was not required, as they were 'watching a stolen TV set!'

Some quotes from car accident insurance forms – reveal further, our ability to excuse ourselves from taking full responsibility. "My car was legally parked as it backed into the other vehicle" and "I collided with a stationary vehicle coming the other way."

Jesus told a parable about a 'Great Banquet' that addressed this matter of excuses. (Luke 14:15-24) God reveals that 'everyone' is invited to the Banquet – to enjoy His blessings now, and also to be at Christ's Banquet in heaven at the end of our days. Today; Jesus still calls out, "Come follow me!" What will our answer and response be to His invitation to us?

In the parable, the people's excuses for not being able to attend the banquet started rolling in. "I have just bought a field, and I must go and see it. Please excuse me." Another said "I have just bought five yoke of oxen, and I'm on my way to try them out. Please excuse me." And yet another said, "I just got married and need to get home to my wife."

At times our excuses may seem more like 'justified reasons' – but when Jesus calls us, we must heed and follow Him.

There were many people mentioned in the Bible who desired to follow Jesus, but had other things they wanted to do first. (Read Luke 9:57-62)

As we make God's Word and ways our first priority; He will enable and guide us to fulfil our other responsibilities, faithfully and effectively – in our work, families and communities.

Jesus said "Steep your life in God-reality, God initiative, God provisions. Don't worry about missing out. You'll find all your everyday human concerns will be met." (Matthew 6:33 –The Message Bible)

EXTRA!

The call of Jesus – is top priority

28

New Birth Day

It is always nice to do something special or different on your birthday. When I am working during the day on my birthday – I look forward to going out to celebrate in the evening by having a meal at our local Bistro.

With my birthday being in June – it reminded me that the Queen also celebrates her 'official' birthday in this month. Her actual birthday is April 21st, but she has her Official Birthday Parade (known as the Trooping of the Colour) on a Saturday in June – when there is a greater likelihood of the weather being good.

The Bible speaks about how it is possible for each one of us to have 'two birthdays!' John records in his gospel – a conversation that Jesus had with a Pharisee named Nicodemus.

Jesus said "I tell you the truth; unless a man is born again (from above) he cannot see the kingdom of God." (John 3:3) Although Nicodemus was a man of great learning – he was confused and replied "Surely he cannot enter a second time into his mother's womb to be born?" Jesus went on to explain that he was not talking about physical birth but a 'spiritual rebirth.' Peter the apostle proclaimed that God – "In His great mercy has given us new birth into a living hope through the resurrection of Jesus Christ from the dead… for you have been born again… through the living and enduring word of God." (1 Peter 1:3, 23)

I can recall the day (14th September 1975) – when I had just turned 18, when I experienced my rebirth day. I realised I needed to ask Jesus to forgive me of my sinfulness and turn from those things that were not pleasing to God – and trust Him to lead and keep me every day of my life as I followed Him.

I made that prayer, and through faith in Christ experienced the peace, joy and excitement that Jesus gives when we are born again by His Spirit. Paul the apostle said "Therefore, if anyone is in Christ, he is a new creation, the old has gone, the new has come." (2 Corinthians 5:17)

God offers each of us, a new start and a new-birth day – through His Son Jesus Christ. We can be free from the guilt and shame of our past sin and can start over again. That is the greatest birthday celebration anyone could ever have!

EXTRA!

In Jesus Christ the old has gone – the new has come.

Who can I turn to?

I have often heard reminders on the TV and radio, asking people not to dial 999 to request Services that are not classed as emergencies. This ensures urgent calls are answered and help is sent – to where there is danger to life, risk of injury and where crimes are in progress.

The London Fire Brigade disclosed the nature of some of the 'so called' emergency requests they had received. Someone asked for help as there was 'a spider crawling on a pillow' and another because 'a mobile phone had been dropped into a toilet.' A woman had called for assistance, after she threw water at fighting dogs – forgetting her dentures were in the glass!

For those of us who have had to call upon an Emergency Service – we will appreciate the support, comfort and skills offered by those who came to help us.

There are also many other 'non emergency' things in life that can cause us to worry, feel stressed and be concerned – and we can lose perspective.

God has blessed us with community. We are here to help, guide and listen to one another in times of need – but in addition, God wants us to call upon Him. He is the God who understands, cares and is interested in everything about us.

Nahum the prophet said "The Lord is good, a refuge in times of trouble. He cares for those who trust in Him…" (Nahum 1:7a)

The great privilege of prayer is – as we share our anxiousness and concerns with God, He grants to us His comfort and consolation.

Peter the apostle wrote, "Give all your worries and cares to God, for He cares what happens to you." (1 Peter 5:7 – New Living Translation)

Giving our cares to God means we need to leave the outcome with Him. He knows the beginning from the end. He sees the big picture in our lives, even when we can't see beyond today.

To those that turn to God – love Him and His ways, and trust Him with everything and in everything – He gives an amazing promise. " .. in all things – God works for the good." (Romans 8:28) God can bring peace into fear, light into darkness, joy into sorrow, and hope into despair.

EXTRA!

God sees the big picture even when we can't see beyond today

30

Car recall

The second-hand car we bought some years ago has generally been very reliable and served us well. We usually take it to our local garage to be serviced – but over the years we have owned it, we have received 2 letters from the main dealer asking us to make an appointment for a 'vehicle recall' re safety concerns.

The last letter informed us there was a possibility the steering wheel fixing bolt may not have been sufficiently tightened during manufacture, and this could potentially lead to excessive play in the steering wheel.

It was reassuring to have this looked at without cost – although my initial thought was one of surprise as the car was nearly 10 years old, and this possible defect had only just been identified.

To 'recall' – means to summon back or return to a place. This reminded me how through the years of my life, God has called me to himself, and continues to call me back to the place where I follow His commands and trust in the promises of His never failing Word.

We can become side-tracked with selfishness and lose our focus in adversity; but whatever may need changing in our attitudes – or whatever comes against us – God will be there for us, when we choose to return to Him.

Throughout the Bible, there is a call for individuals, communities and nations to return to the Lord. The prophet Hosea said "You must return to your God; maintain love and justice and wait for your God always." (Hosea 12:6)

The writer of Lamentations says "Let us examine our ways and test them, and let us return to the Lord." (Lamentations 3:40)

As we read the scriptures – God continues to show us areas of our lives that He wants to change – that will be best for us, and be pleasing to Him. God has made us. His word is our manual for life – and He promises to keep and guide us in all our ways.

Our car was recalled because it needed the expertise of those who made it – to fix it!

Jeremiah the prophet declared from the Lord, "If you return – I will restore you…" (Jeremiah 15:19)

EXTRA!

**Trust God –
He can fix us in our
brokenness**

Commend or complain

While taking a few days holiday in the City of Bath, my wife and I went for an evening meal at a Bar which we had discovered on a previous visit.

The young lady who served us was very polite and enthusiastic – and in conversation, we found out it was her first day at work at this Diner.

We expressed our appreciation for her good service to us as she brought food and drink to our table. Later, when I ordered a cappuccino; she said, "I hope it's alright – it's the first one I've made." I replied, "It looks fine." As I drank it – the froth continued. It was mostly milk with only a hint of coffee flavour at the bottom of the cup! (but it tasted OK)

My thought was – "We've complimented and encouraged the waitress on her first day in a new job – do I now have to inform her that her coffee making isn't fine."

Thinking back to my first weeks in work; I went with my heart and said nothing – choosing to leave her with my comments that commended, rather than complain.

Each day we will meet people who are longing to be uplifted and encouraged – by our words and actions that show affirmation and appreciation. In their struggles, dilemmas and feelings of being down-hearted, we can 'pour courage' back into their lives.

The author of the book of Hebrews in the Bible told believers to "encourage one another daily" (Hebrews 3:13-14) – so they could walk the walk, and talk the talk of their faith – firmly and confidently all their days.

We all face those times when we need to persevere and not give up – but without encouragement, without someone cheering us on, it can be difficult.

Later on in Hebrews, the question is asked "…let us consider how we may spur one another on towards love and good deeds." The answer is: – We need one another. The Church was told to keep meeting together and encourage one another – and all the more… (Read Hebrews 10:24-25)

This week – may we be aware of those God given opportunities to impart courage and confidence to someone. Choosing to commend them in some way; rather than complain, can make a world of difference – one life at a time.

EXTRA!

Encourage others – daily!

All things are possible

I'm amazed at the skill of carpet fitters as they put down floor coverings – laying them perfectly to the edge of skirting boards and cutting them to fit around other units in a room. Each time I have attempted to lay a small carpet – I have always been left with a few small gaps to fill around the edges. Any carpet we buy now – I am happy (and so is my wife) – that we get it fitted by the experts!

Like with most things; what we find extremely difficult – would become possible with commitment and practice. So often we can limit ourselves by thinking that something is impossible for us to accomplish.

When we face difficult and seemingly impossible situations in our lives, we can draw strength and encouragement from the Bible – that reveals to us that God is the God of the impossible.

Jeremiah the prophet prayed to the Lord saying, "Ah, Sovereign Lord, You have made the heavens and the earth by your great power and outstretched arm. Nothing is too hard for you." (Jeremiah 32:17)

I may not be able to do all things well (like carpet fitting or cooking!) but God always gives us His ability to do the things that He calls us to do. Where God guides us – He will provide for us.

Jesus said "Everything is possible for him who believes." (Mark 9:23) This does not guarantee that we will get everything we want – but when we believe (with child-like faith) and pray what God has promised in His word – He will give to us all that we need to do His work and bring glory to His name.

The author of Hebrews reminds us that "Without faith it is impossible to please God, because anyone who comes to him must believe that He exists." (Hebrews 11:6)

It brings delight to God's heart, when we hand over those impossible looking circumstances to Him – and trust Him for the outcome.

The Bible is loaded with stories that will remind us that God brings about the impossible and miraculous for His people and through His people – not just in history, but also for us each day.

> **EXTRA!**
>
> God equips and enables us to do the things He calls us to do

Shadows

I was walking to work one afternoon during a sunny interval – in between all the rain showers we had been having. The sun was bright, and as I turned around, I noticed my shadow behind me was very long.

It reminded me of the fun times we had when our daughter was younger – when we went over to a nearby park in the evening and walked in front of the coloured light illuminations, and cast huge shadows of ourselves across the grass.

In addition to being fun – shadows can also make us feel scared. Shadows in their nature are obscure and can cause a fear of the unknown. (This is why film directors use them to create panic within the viewing audience)

When something is not clear and we can't see what is going on – our thoughts can take over and make things seem alot worse than what is most likely to happen.

We all have those times in life when we feel we are walking in the shadows – when an outcome is difficult, the outlook uncertain and when doubts and anxiety cast their long shadows across the brightness of our day.

David the psalmist wrote the words of the well known Psalm 23. As a shepherd, he would have had some shadow experiences on those nights watching over his father's sheep.

David said of God "Even though I walk through the valley of the shadow of death (or the darkest valley) I will fear no evil for You are with me…" (Psalm 23:4)

There was a shadow in David's life that he welcomed and rejoiced about. When David had to flee from Saul and hid in a cave he said to God "I will take refuge in the shadow of your wings until the disaster has passed." (Psalm 57:1b)

David's trust was in His God; who was his helper – and while he was in the desert of Judah he proclaimed "I sing in the shadow of your wings. I stay close to you; your right hand upholds me." (Psalm 63:7-8)

If you are journeying through a shadow season at this time – remember that God walks with you and watches over you. Whether we are experiencing a cave of darkness or a desert of doubt; we can call upon God, the Father of the heavenly lights, who does not change like shifting shadows." (James 1:16b) and He will grant us His peace and presence amidst our fears.

EXTRA!

The Lord is with you in the shadows of life

Roots

One summer, my wife and I decided upon a project to revitalize our front garden. We had 5 large shrubs we wanted to remove so we could plant out some new varieties. The cutting down of the old shrubs was quite easy – but the removal of their root systems gave us a tough challenge (and plenty of physical exercise!)

As we dug down, we found some large root balls had grown tightly against the garden wall. As we pulled at the smaller roots – they began to lift up the surrounding lawn.

Roots are vital when it comes to growing healthy trees and shrubs – but those same roots can become a major problem when it comes to removing them.

The Bible speaks about aspects in our lives that need to be 'rooted in' – and also things that we need to 'root out.'

Jeremiah the prophet said "…Blessed is the man who trusts in the Lord, whose confidence is in Him. He will be like a tree planted by the water that sends out its roots by the stream." (Jeremiah 17:7-8) When our life is rooted in God and His word – He becomes our strength in the heat of our fears, and refreshes us when we are lost in the wilderness of worry.

As we continue to live Christ's way – we will be rooted and built up in Him and strengthened in our faith. (Colossians 2:6-7)

Just as a shrub or plant relies on its roots for water and nutrients – we can draw on God's power and resources to help us grow in the ways that He desires for us.

The apostle Paul prayed that the believers in Ephesus would be "rooted and established in love." (Ephesians 3:16-17) God wants His amazing and immeasurable love towards us – to be evident in all we do and say.

Just as tree roots can become diseased and prevent growth and fruitfulness – we also need to watch out for those motives and desires, like envy and pride – that will affect us if we don't root them out.

The writer of Hebrews said "See to it… that no bitter root grows up to cause trouble and defile many." (Hebrews 12:15)

EXTRA!

Be rooted and established in love

35

New Identity

I had just received a new 'identity badge' as an employee of the school where I work. The wording on the lanyard reminded me I was part of 'an 11-18 school' – and my name and title of Invigilator identified me with my role and responsibilities.

Identity is a big issue – covering aspects like knowing who we are and how others see us. It is defined as the qualities and beliefs that make a person or group different from others.

The most unique thing in the world is the human fingerprint. Even identical twins have different fingerprints. If we burned our skin or got a wound on our finger tips; fingerprints will not change – as the new skin grows to the exact same pattern. Fingerprints are one of the best ways to identify a person.

From God's perspective – we are all unique. There is only one you, and there will never be anyone like you again. God has unique plans for each of us. He reveals those purposes to us – as we seek Him.

We often hear of people experiencing an 'identity crisis' where they are not sure of who they are – or their place and purpose in society.

Many things can come against us in life where we can lose our focus and sense of direction.

When we live by God's word – we discover a new identity which is found in Jesus Christ alone.

Paul the apostle put it like this. "Therefore, if anyone is in Christ, he is a new creation. The old has passed away – the new has come." (2 Corinthians 5:17) He went on to say "For in Christ Jesus you are all sons of God through faith…" (Galatians 3:26)

Our identity; no longer needs to be defined by the mistakes we have made in the past or present. When we confess our sins to God and turn from them – He forgives us completely and remembers them no more. Paul reminds us that God is the one who takes away our guilt and shame. "Therefore, there is now no condemnation for those who are in Christ Jesus…" (Romans 8:1)

God offers to each of us – the privilege and identity of being His children. John's gospel reminds us that "…to all who did receive Him, who believed in His name, He gave the right to become children of God…" (John 1:12)

EXTRA!

God has a unique plan and purpose just for you

36

Friends

In the early years of social networking – using the 'Friends Reunited' website – it was good to be able to make contact with some school friends that I had not been in touch with for over thirty years.

Thinking about friendship, I was reminded of two TV programmes. The theme tune of 'Friends' says – "I'll be there for you, (when the rain starts to pour) – I'll be there for you, (like I've been there before) – I'll be there for you, 'cause you're there for me too."

The Neighbours theme tune ends with – "Neighbours, should be there for one another. That's when good neighbours become good friends." True friends are always there for each other.

Solomon wrote – "Friends love through all kinds of weather, and families stick together in all kinds of trouble." (Proverbs 17:17 – The Message Bible)

Community was God's design for each of us to 'have friends' and also 'be a friend' to others.

One day, Jesus was teaching His disciples about the importance of obeying His commands and remaining in His love. He then went on to mention an amazing truth about how He calls us His friends.

Jesus said – "You are my friends if you do what I command. I no longer call you servants, because a servant does not know his master's business. Instead, I have called you friends, for everything I learned from my Father I have made known to you." (John 15:14-15)

To be a friend of God is the greatest friendship and relationship that we can experience. To those that seek Him – He reveals His heart and purposes to them.

God doesn't just want us to know about Him (that is knowledge) but wants us to 'know Him' as a Friend. (that is relationship)

If you are going through a time, where even your best friends have let you down – or you are feeling alone in your circumstances – remember that 'God is a friend who sticks even closer than a brother.' Speak to Him in prayer – He will be there for you.

> **EXTRA!**
>
> True friends are always there for each other

37

What brings you joy?

I had just treated myself to a bar of chocolate from a vending machine. On the outer wrapper I read the words "What brings you joy? Win it – made out of chocolate!" It went on to say "find a pink wrapped bar and you have won a chocolate sculpture of your choice." (Mine would be a chocolate guitar!)

The question caused me to reflect on what true joy is all about. The joy that God wants us to experience in our lives – is not based on what we feel and is not dependent upon our circumstances.

Happiness can be seen as an outward expression – in a smile or a laugh – but even these can be temporary. God desires that we know His joy as a lasting experience – where we have inner peace and contentment regardless of our circumstances. This is the joy God gives to those that seek after Him.

Jesus told a parable. "The kingdom of heaven is like treasure hidden in a field. When a man found it, he hid it again, and then 'in his joy' went and sold all he had and bought that field." (Matthew 13:44) Lasting joy comes from knowing God's plan for our lives and then pursuing His purposes in all our ways – with all that we have.

David the Psalmist had sought God's direction and knew joy was to be found in God himself. He wrote "You have made known to me the path of life; you will fill me with joy in your presence, with eternal pleasures at your right hand." (Psalm 16:11)

True joy also comes from giving to, and serving others, rather than seeking what we can get for ourselves.

Luke quotes the words of the apostle Paul when he wrote in the Book of Acts – "In everything I did, I showed you that by this kind of hard work we must help the weak, remembering the words the Lord Jesus himself said:"It is more blessed to give than to receive."(Acts 20:35)

What is your answer to the question "What brings you joy?" The prophet Nehemiah reminds us that "…the joy of the Lord is your strength." (Nehemiah 8:10)

The authentic joy that God gives – in knowing Him: will keep your heart and mind in peace and hope, through the seasons of crisis and challenge.

> **EXTRA!**
>
> **Draw strength from the joy God gives**

38

Inconvenient Interruptions

I was on my way down to Church to carry out my duties as Marriage Registrar at a wedding. I always leave in good time on these occasions, so I can set out all the stationery items required.

As I looked to cross a road, I noticed a man who had fallen. I went to his aid. He was conscious but shaken. He didn't require an ambulance – but I did start to think that if I had to stay with him for any length of time; I was going to run the risk of being late to prepare for my vital role at the Wedding. For each of us – life will bring its inconvenient interruptions!

However, it is at times like this – when we are most needed by others. Those circumstances that break into our schedules – although inconvenient, are opportunities to show people love, care and compassion.

Jesus always made time for people – even when he was tired and busy. One day, the apostles gathered round Jesus and reported to him all they had done and taught. They had not even had a chance to eat.

Jesus said to them "Come with me by yourselves to a quiet place and get some rest." Their time of relaxing was disturbed as thousands followed them. This interruption led to the miracle of Jesus feeding more than 5000 people with five loaves and two fish. They all ate and were satisfied. (Read the full story in Mark 6:30-44)

On another occasion – Jesus had just received news that John the Baptist had been beheaded in prison.

On hearing this, He withdrew by boat privately to a solitary place – but the crowds followed him. When Jesus saw the large crowd, he had compassion on them and healed their sick. (Matthew 14:13-14)

At a time when Jesus needed quietness to reflect – He still gave of himself to others when they came to Him.

Interruptions need to be seen as part of our day – not as an intrusion. God always wants to use us to bring His hope and help to people in need.

> **EXTRA!**
>
> **Interruptions are opportunities to serve others**

Weather warning

On Thursday 24th October 2013, the Met Office issued a warning of potentially damaging winds across the southern parts of England – 5 days ahead of the storm. This became known as the 'St Jude's Day' storm. It battered the southern part of the UK on Monday 28th October and caused widespread disruption. Over 100 flood warnings and alerts were given across the country and the 70-80mph winds brought down trees and left 625,000 households without power. The highest recorded speed of these hurricane winds was 99mph off the Isle of Wight.

Due to an accurate forecast and warnings being issued people opted to work from home that day. Councils cleared drains of leaves the day before and had staff on stand-by to help. Train services were cancelled to avoid the danger of trees on the line.

One outcome of giving these warnings; was that Insurers received fewer claims as people took action to protect their property against the wind. I recall moving my wheelie bin and plastic flower pots from the garden, into the garage at that time!

Through every book of the Bible, God warns us of many things we should avoid, to keep us from causing harm and pain to ourselves and others – and points us to how we can experience His peace, purpose and blessing each day of our lives.

King David wrote "The ordinances (commands) of the Lord are sure and altogether righteous… By them is your servant warned; in keeping them there is great reward." (Psalm 19:11)

God's word is perfect – it will revive us – giving us new hope. His statutes are trustworthy and we will grow in wisdom as we practice them. The Lord's precepts are right and they will bring joy to our heart. The commandments of the Lord are pure – they will enlighten our eyes. (Read Psalm 19:7-10)

Asaph the psalmist said "Hear, O my people, and I will warn you – if you would but listen to me… (Psalm 81:8)

As we heed God's word and warnings – we will find that walking His path gives us security, shelter and protection.

EXTRA!

God's warnings in His word are for our benefit and blessing

40

Take a pause!

When I'm Exam Invigilating – I frequently notice with some subjects; how a good number of students start writing their answers almost immediately after the exam has commenced.

Although they are given plenty of time – rather than looking through the whole paper, reading questions and instructions carefully and pausing to give thought before writing – students are still keen to start filling in the answer pages.

As I observed this, I was reminded of a Hebrew Bible word that is used in the book of Psalms on more than 70 occasions. The word is 'Selah.' Although it is difficult to translate and can have several implications – the Amplified Bible translates it as 'pause – and calmly think of that.'

We live in a busy and instant culture. We can get anything from instant meals, instant insurance quotes and instant loans – and through using email and texts, we expect instant replies and acknowledgements.

Many of us will probably remember occasions when we replied quickly to a phone message or email without giving our answer or wording some careful thought.

Taking time to pause before responding, allows us to get perspective and think through what we may say or write to someone, so there is no mis-understanding.

In the Bible – the use of the word Selah; follows many comments made by the psalmist, asking the reader to 'stop and listen' – pause, meditate and reflect.

David the psalmist wrote – "With my voice I cry to the Lord, and He hears and answers me… Selah! (Psalm 3:4)

He said of God – "You are a hiding place for me; You, Lord, preserve me from trouble, You surround me with songs and shouts of deliverance." Selah! (Psalm 32:7)

"The Lord of hosts is with us; the God of Jacob is our Refuge (our High Tower and Stronghold) Selah! (Psalm 46:11)

As you start a new week – choose to pause in the midst of the busy times and reflect on the greatness of God's saving power and the goodness of His promises. God is ready to listen – and will direct us in every circumstance and conversation, as we acknowledge Him. "Selah – pause and calmly think of that!"

> **EXTRA!**
>
> Take time – to reflect on the greatness and goodness of God

41

Forever

A few years ago I bought my wife a bunch of carnation flowers which we put in a vase in our lounge. Remarkably – they were still looking healthy and colourful up to 5 weeks later. This was good for us – but not so beneficial for the florist trade!

Sometimes we pick a rose from the garden; but like most flowers – once picked, they will not live long.

In the Bible, the prophet Isaiah makes a reference to flowers fading and not lasting. He said -"The grass withers and the flowers fall, but the word of our God stands for ever." (Isaiah 40:8) King Solomon declared "I know that everything God does will endure for ever; nothing can be added to it and nothing taken from it…" (Ecclesiastes 3:14)

We may be familiar with the quote – "All good things must come to an end." This was written by Geoffrey Chaucer in 1374 (who is considered to be the greatest English poet of the Middle Ages) – but the word 'good' was added centuries later.

However – God wants us to enjoy good blessings, like His love, joy and peace – every day of our lives. His mercies never come to an end – they are new every morning, and it is these things God wants us to experience – even through the sad and difficult situations of life that come to us all. He is our hope for today, the future, and forever.

David the psalmist wrote a song for the dedication of the temple. He understood about the Lord's lasting purposes when he wrote "…His anger lasts only a moment, but His favour lasts a lifetime, weeping may remain for a night, but rejoicing comes in the morning." (Psalm 30:5)

The things that God wants to do in and through our lives will be lasting – for He is the God whose love endures forever, and who is forever faithful and forever true to His Word.

> **EXTRA!**
>
> **Everything God does will endure forever**

42

Messages

On the 3rd December 1992, the first SMS (Short Message Service – known as a text) was sent. An engineer wrote a message (saying 'Happy Christmas') – and sent it from a PC to a mobile device. Today, most of us, keep in touch by sending updates and messages via our mobile phone or computer. The pioneer of SMS – Matti Makkonen, did not patent his invention, because he didn't think it was a patentable innovation!

My telephone answering service always reminds me of the number of new messages I have to listen to, and my email server informs me of my new messages that are unread. With my phone, I can listen to messages again, save or delete them. With emails – I can either delete, or transfer them to various folders for future reference.

The Bible is God's complete message to each of us – which He wants us to read, heed and respond to. When Paul wrote his letter to all in Rome he reminded them that "…faith comes from hearing the message, and the message is heard through the word of Christ." (Romans 10:17)

John specifically high-lighted some key messages when he wrote "This is the message we have from Him and declare to you: God is light; in Him there is no darkness at all… but if we walk in the light, as He is in the light… the blood of Jesus, His Son purifies us from every sin." (1 John 1:5, 7)

Later on in his letter John reminds us, "This is the message you heard from the beginning: We should love one another." (1 John 3:11) We can love – because God first loved us. (See 1 John 4:19) Jesus reveals by His own example everything that He asks of us.

We can walk in the light of God's message in the Bible; because Jesus said, "I am the light of the world" and He promised that whoever follows Him – will never walk in darkness, but will have the light of life." (John 8:12)

The messages that God sends through His word to each of us, are life giving and life changing – bringing hope and healing to our brokenness.

My SMS to us all this week is "Check out the fullness and greatness of God's message to you; read one of the gospels in the Bible – and discover the bigger picture for your life."

EXTRA!

In God's Word you will find a message from Him – to you

Seasons

In 2014 – we experienced some extreme variation in seasonal temperatures. We had a record breaking cold spring – but our summer season was the ninth warmest since records began in 1910 – and gave us 588 hours of sunshine.

We also had a prolonged heat-wave in the middle of July where temperatures regularly reached 30C (86F) and the most sustained period of hot weather since July 2006.

Autumn arrives and we see the evidence of changing seasons. Nights draw in – and I find myself walking into spider cobwebs. (Not indoors! – but when I walk in the garden). Crane flies enter the house uninvited – and condensation starts to form on the window glass overnight. Each season brings its joys and challenges.

Life is very much like changing seasons. Our personal circumstances can change without warning – and when least expected. We can have times (even years) when everything is going 'just fine' and other seasons when the difficulties and 'tough times' just keep coming.

King Solomon wrote "There is a time for everything, and a season for every activity under heaven." (Ecclesiastes 3:1, 17) "and a time for every deed."

Whatever 'life season' you are in today – draw strength from David the Psalmist, who turned to God and said "My times are in your hands…" (Psalm 31:15)

He went on to say "…for You are my fortress, my refuge in times of trouble." (Psalm 59:16)…" Trust in Him at all times…" (Psalm 62:8)

In my own life – I can look back on times of bereavement and loss, sickness, redundancy, unemployment and disappointment; but as I've looked to God and His word – He has brought about the change in those seasons- bringing me His peace, hope, healing, strength and direction.

It is during those difficult times, that I learn more about patience, obedience and faith in God – who is good and faithful to His promises.

This week: "May the Lord of peace himself give you His peace at all times and in every way." (2 Thessalonians 3:16)

EXTRA!

Your times are in God's hands

44

The Voice

Many of us will have watched on TV the programme called *'The Voice'* – where four well known music celebrities search for the nation's top vocal talent.

In series 3 – Kylie Minogue, will.i.am, Sir Tom Jones and Ricky Wilson were the coaches who listen to the contestants – in chairs facing opposite the stage to avoid seeing them.

The programme is all about the 'voice' and not what the artist looks like or brings to their performance visually. If the coach likes 'what they hear' – they press a button to rotate their chair to signify they are interested in working with that person.

I'm always interested to listen to how the coaches describe the voice of the contestants – using adjectives like amazing, beautiful, emotional, incredible or powerful.

The human voice is the greatest musical instrument that God made – for His pleasure and ours – and His Word, the Bible, is the 'Voice of God.' In the beginning when God spoke – everything came into being. When God said, "Let there be light." – there was light. (Genesis 1:3)

King David informs us – "The voice of the Lord is powerful… and majestic." (Psalm 29:4) The Bible is different to any other book – because when we read it, we will hear God's voice.

He uses His living word; to speak to us, and reveals how we can know Him personally, through His Son Jesus Christ.

Moses pleaded with the Israelites to "...choose life... and love the Lord your God, listen to his voice and hold fast to him." (Deuteronomy 30:20)

When it comes to singing – many of us would not want to sing solo in public and have our voices heard, but God hears – any and every voice that calls out to Him.

The psalmist wrote, "Hear my voice when I call, O Lord; be merciful to me and answer… Your face will I seek." (Psalm 27:7-8)

When we pray like that and our eyes are ever on the Lord – God will hear our voice and turn and be gracious to us. (Psalm 26:16)

EXTRA!

Listen for God's voice – He is longing to speak with you

Precious

When I was walking through town, I noticed my local bank had a new advertising logo on their front window which read – "Protect what's precious to you.'

It reminded me that precious things are of great value – and they must not be wasted or treated carelessly.

People, family and friends are precious, and we need to put continued effort into maintaining good relationships.

Memories are precious – because they remind us of good times and lessons learnt, and our time is very precious – so we must use it wisely.

The Bible also informs us of others things that are precious. David the psalmist said of God's ordinances and commands – "they are more precious than pure gold… by them is your servant warned…"

God's law and statutes are precious because they make us wise, give joy to the heart and revive us. (Read Psalm 19:7-11)

Another precious thing to King David; was that He understood how well he was known about – by God. He declared;"How precious to me are your thoughts, O God! How vast is the sum of them! Were I to count them, they would outnumber the grains of sand…" (Psalm 139:17-18a)

What was precious to David – to the point of being incomprehensible and overwhelming was that he was contrasting his knowledge of God with God's knowledge of him.

God; who knows and understands us so well – is the One we can trust in every circumstance of life.

As we consider that offer to protect what is precious to us – let us also remember the words of David's prayer when he asked of God "…may your love and your truth always protect me." (Psalm 40:11)

The LORD is a shield to those whose walk is blameless, for He guards the course of the just and protects the way of His faithful ones." (Proverbs 2:7-8) These are great and precious promises from God – to you!

> **EXTRA!**
>
> **God's promises to you are both great and precious**

46

Benefits

I received a letter reminding me that my car breakdown service was due for renewal very soon. The enclosed leaflet had a picture of an ornate gold front door – and the advertising logo read, 'Come in for your gold benefits.' As I read through the letter it went on to say – 'log-in to view all your benefits!'

We all enjoy benefits that help towards our well-being, bring us enjoyment or are an advantage for us. One of my first jobs when I left school was selling electrical appliances. I received training on how to highlight the features of an appliance that would benefit the customer by meeting their needs.

David the psalmist spoke about the benefits that he enjoyed by knowing God. He said – "Praise the Lord, O my soul, and forget not all his benefits. He forgives all my sins and heals all my diseases; He redeems my life from the pit and crowns me with love and compassion. He satisfies my desires with good things, so that my youth is renewed…" (Psalm 103:2-5)

In remembering and acknowledging God's benefits and blessings towards us, we are to thank God for who He is – and not just for what He does for us.

All of God's benefits are acts of His kindness, goodness and mercy – that He bestows on us. God's benefits and plans for us are always good – all of the time.

Sometimes when our prayers are not answered and life's circumstances are hard to understand, we must continue to look to God – who knows how to work things out in ways that are best for us – ways that will strengthen our faith, teach patience, deepen trust and build character.

If you are in need of some encouragement today – open up a Bible and start reading. You will soon discover how you can experience God's benefits of forgiveness, peace, purpose, strength, satisfaction, and joy…

EXTRA!

Thank God for who He is – not just for what He does

47

New home

Our daughter and son in law had just moved into their new home in Wales when my wife and I visited them. During the few days we spent with them, we became experts in assembling flat packed furniture, recycling packaging, emptying boxes and moving household items carefully up and down stairways!

It's good to move to a new home and area – meet new friends and neighbours, become part of the community and get to visit new places. Moving house will always be an opportunity for new beginnings.

The Bible is a message about the new start that God offers to each of us. The writer of Lamentations acknowledged "…His compassions never fail. They are new every morning; great is your faithfulness." (Lamentations 3:22-23)

God's purpose in sending His Son Jesus to the world was to reconcile us to himself.

The apostle Paul explains what happened when Jesus gave himself for our sinfulness and the outcome of choosing to live life for God, and not for ourselves. He wrote – "Therefore, if anyone is in Christ, he is a new creation; the old has gone, the new has come!" All this is from God, who reconciled us to himself through Christ" (2 Corinthians 5:17-18)

Whatever problems or decisions we face – we can experience new hope and a new purpose in Christ.

We may not be able to change our circumstances, but as we read God's word, He will guide and strengthen us, and give us a new and right attitude towards everything that comes our way.

The new life and new start – that God desires for us, is where we "take on an entirely new way of life – a God-fashioned life, a life renewed from the inside and working itself into your conduct as God accurately reproduces His character in you." (Ephesians 4:23-24 – The Message Bible)

Whatever the past holds over us; and whatever the future holds for us, through forgiveness and repentance 'in Christ' – He wipes our slate clean and offers us a new start in life.

> **EXTRA!**
>
> **God's compassions never fail. They are new every morning**

48

Bullworker

I was in my late teens when I made a purchase of a "Bullworker." The Bullworker; which was invented in Germany in 1953 – is an Isometric exercise device used for strengthening specific muscle groups in the body. Isometric exercises – require you to tense your muscles without actually moving any part of your body.

The manufacturer instruction booklet explains that you need only use 60% of your strength for the exercises shown – and this is sufficient to increase strength and build up muscles rapidly.

Although I still have my Bullworker, (and exercise wall chart!) it has not been used for years as I've chosen more gentle forms of exercise.

Physical health, strength and fitness is important to us all – but not even a Bullworker can help when it comes to 'finding the strength we need' to face and deal with daily challenges that can come into our lives.

The Message Bible puts the words of Paul from 1 Timothy 4:8 like this. "Workouts in the gymnasium are useful, but a disciplined life in God is far more so, making you fit both today and forever."

The psalmist proclaimed "God is our refuge and strength, an ever present help in trouble." (Psalm 46:1)

The prophet Isaiah also testified to the strength that the Lord gives to us when he wrote – "He gives strength to the weary and increases the power of the weak. Even youths grow tired and weary, and young men stumble and fall; but those who hope in the LORD will renew their strength. They will soar on wings like eagles; they will run and not grow weary, they will walk and not be faint." (Isaiah 40:29-31)

The apostle Paul experienced what it was to be alone. At the time of his trial, he could find no witnesses who would take his side.

However, when everyone had deserted him – he declares with confidence "…But the Lord stood at my side and gave me strength." (2 Timothy 4:17) Today, He will be your strength also – when you reach out to Him.

EXTRA!

Those who hope in the Lord will renew their strength

49

Gifts

Christmas is fast approaching – and most of us will have done some shopping, as we look for that perfect gift to give to our family and friends. A Christmas spending intentions survey suggested the UK total festive spend will be around 22.3 billion pounds. Gifts make up the majority of that estimate, followed by food and drink and then trees and decorations.

Another survey revealed that gadgets and 'tech based' gifts are more popular than the traditional presents of jewellery, clothing and perfume. Sadly, millions of pounds are spent on presents classed as 'unwanted' – and end up in the back of a cupboard.

Most people link the giving of gifts at Christmas with the Kings visit to Jesus – when they brought Him gold, frankincense and myrrh.

The Wise Men (known as Magi) came from the east asking – "Where is the One who has been born King of the Jews? We saw his star in the east and have come to worship him."(Matthew 2:2)

Many Christmas cards show the kings at the nativity, when in fact they did not arrive until Jesus was nearly two years old. "On coming to the house, they saw the child with his mother Mary…" (Matthew 2:11)

The Magi had chosen and brought meaningful and significant gifts – but before giving them; they fulfilled the reason for their visit – "they bowed down and worshipped Him. Then they opened their treasures and presented Him with gifts…"

Gold was associated with kings. In Revelation 19:16 – Jesus is named as the "King of Kings and Lord of Lords." Frankincense – a perfume connected with worship, symbolised the divinity of Jesus. The psalmist wrote "Come let us bow down in worship, let us kneel before the Lord our Maker for He is our God…" (Psalm 95:6-7) Myrrh (which was used to put on cloths to wrap bodies for burial) reminds us that Jesus was born to die. "…He appeared so that He might take away our sins…" (1 John 3:5)

Christina Rossetti wrote the words for the carol "In the bleak Mid-Winter." In the last verse she reminds us what we can give to Jesus. "If I were a wise man I would do my part: Yet what I can I give Him, give my heart." As we give ourselves to following Jesus – we receive life's greatest and precious gift – "…the gift of God is eternal life through Christ Jesus our Lord." (Romans 6:23)

EXTRA!

Jesus – God's most precious gift to the world

Catseyes

A few years ago we had a new garage built. Our old one had wooden doors; but the new one has an up and over door that is brilliant white in colour. I have noticed on several occasions when it is dark – the brightness of the moon reflects off the garage door and lights up our driveway.

Reflected light can be useful and even life-saving. In 1934, Percy Shaw patented his invention of the Catseye reflective road marker. A Catseye is made of 2 pairs of reflective glass spheres – and they have improved road safety as they reflect car lights to help drivers see the road in dark or foggy conditions. Some believe that Percy Shaw invented the Catseye after noticing light reflecting from the eyes of a cat sitting beside a road.

Jesus spoke about how we are to reflect His light. In His Sermon on the Mount He said "You are the light of the world… let your light shine before men, that they may see your good deeds and praise your Father in heaven." (Matthew 5:14, 16)

God wants us to reflect His love, goodness, mercy, kindness and all his other attributes – to those we meet daily and share life with.

The apostle Paul reminded the Church in Corinth "…we all 'reflect' the Lord's glory…" (2 Corinthians 3:18a) The word reflect in this verse may also mean to behold.

As we behold the splendour, majesty and greatness of God as revealed in His word – we become transformed into his likeness with ever increasing glory, which comes from the Lord"… (2 Corinthians 3:18b)

When we look at a bright moon, we are actually seeing the 'reflected light' from the sun bouncing off the moon.

God wants to use us to reflect His Son – Jesus Christ, in this world – bringing His light into dark circumstances, His peace into fearful minds, and His hope into broken lives.

The chorus of a song I wrote many years ago reads: "Take me Lord, and make me Lord, a shining light for You – Take me as I am I ask, and be in all I do – May the love of Jesus shine, from me to others too."

EXTRA!

Jesus – the Light of the World

Every step

I was walking my usual route into town – using the 112 steps which lead down to the main street. Each step is made up of a number of bricks; and on my way I noticed a good quantity of them had been marked with a yellow line.

Taking a closer look – I observed the line had been placed on certain bricks to identify them as being loose, and in need of being re-laid securely.

Both my wife and I have had the experience of stepping on a loose brick on these steps after it has been raining. The result is – water splashes out, and either goes in your shoes or up the back of your leg!

As we walk through life – we will all have times when it feels like we have trodden on a loose brick. Our security can be pulled from under our feet and our confidence and assurance wobbles during difficult situations.

In the Bible – David the psalmist looks to God as the One who is with him on every step of his journey. He declared "My steps have held to your paths; my feet have not slipped." (Psalm 17:5)

In a later psalm, David went on to say "The Lord delights in the way of the man whose steps He has made firm; though he stumble, he will not fall, for the Lord upholds him with His hand." (Psalm 37:23-24)

The writer of Psalm 119 made a deliberate choice of his will, when he chose the path he was going to make his steps upon. He said to God – "I have considered my ways and have turned my steps to your statutes." (Psalm 119:59) He was going to walk in God's direction for his life – where God would walk with him and His word would instruct him.

Just as those bricks on the steps down to the town need to be secured; God secures our steps. If we should falter or stumble – God will lift us onto our feet again as we trust every step of our lives to Him.

EXTRA!

Every step you take – God is watching you

52

Wishing or hoping

It was early in November when we received our first Christmas booklet through our door. A Garden centre was promising me – "they had got everything I could wish for this Christmas!"

I was viewing a current Christmas Advert on TV for a major retail store – and their closing line was "Whatever you wish for this Christmas, make it fabulous this year…"

These two advertisements remind me of the popular Roy Wood song from 1973 when he sang "Well I wish it could be Christmas every day!" On that first Christmas; when God entered our world – it was so we could experience His amazing love, full forgiveness, and perfect peace– 'every day of our lives.'

To wish: is to feel or express a strong desire for something that is not easily attainable – or to want something that cannot or probably will not happen.

In contrast: when the word 'hope' is mentioned in the Bible, it is based on God and His faithfulness, and therefore we can have 'absolute assurance' – that He will be true to what He says in His word. "In His name (Jesus) the nations will put their hope." (Matthew 12:21)

Christmas is all about Jesus Christ – bringing His light and hope into the darkness of our world. God said – "Those who hope in me, will not be disappointed." (Isaiah 49:23b)

Paul describes Jesus as "God's indescribable gift" to the world. He is so amazing, that words are not sufficient to describe Him. (2 Corinthians 9:15)

Shepherds left their flocks to find Him and Magi travelled from afar to worship Him – the One who came to save His people from their sins." (Matthew 1:21)

In 1868 – Phillips Brooks wrote the carol – O little town of Bethlehem. In the last line of the first verse, he reminds us of the confidence and hope that Jesus Christ gives to us. "The hopes and fears of all the years are met in Thee tonight."

Whatever you may be hoping for this Christmas – may the "God of hope fill you with all joy and peace in believing, that you may abound in hope…" (Romans 15:13)

> **EXTRA!**
>
> Those who hope in God – will not be disappointed!

Other Titles by Jim Collins

'Something To Think About'
– Jim's first book of 52 Modern Day Parables.

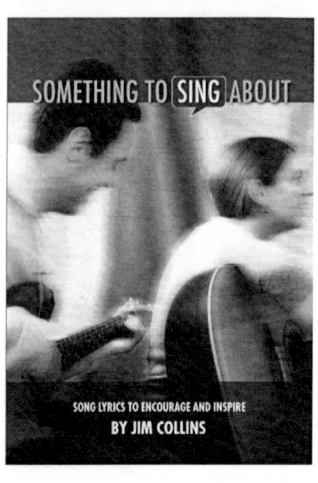

'Something To Sing About' – 40 Christian Lyric songs – that will encourage and inspire you to worship and praise God in your daily living.

To order or for further details, telephone 01803 858340
Or email james.p.collins@btopenworld.com